Copyright: © Daniel Turner

SIMPLE HISTORY

ISBN-13: 978-1537036199

ISBN-10: 153703619X

Part of the Simple guide series

Some images credited: freepik

Written by Daniel Turner & Joshua Kennedy

Illustrator:
Daniel Turner

Editor: Michelle Erb

This title is in United States English.

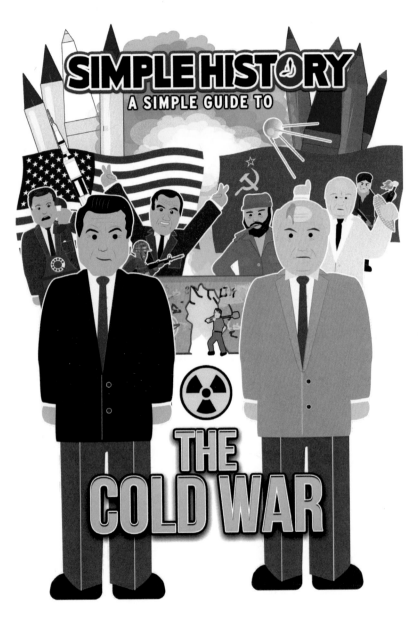

SIMPLE HISTORY

A SIMPLE GUIDE TO

THE COLD WAR

Written by Daniel Turner & Joshua Kennedy
Illustrated by Daniel Turner

CONTENTS

INTRODUCTION

Following the end of World War II, a series of small conflicts and an arms race occurred between the Western and Eastern world, primarily between the United States and the Soviet Union. During these tense times a nuclear war between the two superpowers seemed likely, but was ultimately avoided.

While the United States and the USSR never directly met on the battlefield, the two nations would support small wars around the world to expand and defend their national interests. The two nations would also create alliances with satellite nations for mutual defense and support.

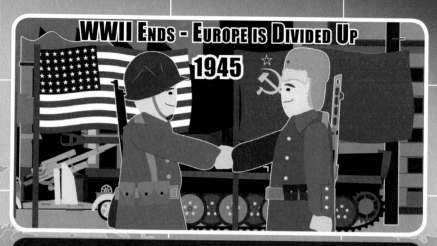

WWII Ends - Europe is Divided Up
1945

Following Nazi Germany's fall, Europe was split up between the Americans and Soviet Russia. Western Europe and the western part of Germany would fall under the control of the United States, Great Britain, and France. Eastern Germany and Eastern Europe would fall under communist control. The city of Berlin would also be split in the same way.

BERLIN AIRLIFT 1948

Half of Berlin was within the Western part of Germany under Soviet control, and half of it was controlled by the United States, France, and Britain. The communist half soon became isolated when the Soviets tightened regulations limiting the import of goods into the city. East Berlin found itself in short supply of resources. A series of airlifts from the United States began to supply the surrounded and cut-off portion of the city with necessities such as food and fuel.

NATO IS ESTABLISHED
1949

For mutual protection and defense, the non-Soviet controlled nations came together and established the North Atlantic Treaty Organization. These nations signed a mutual defense contract, promising to aid each other in case of war.

THE SOVIET UNION TESTS A NUCLEAR BOMB

1949

The Soviet Union detonated a nuclear bomb for the first time in 1949, making it the second nuclear-armed country in the world, after the United States. This marked the beginning of the threat of nuclear war, causing tensions to grow. This first Soviet nuclear bomb was known as "First Lightning", and was roughly the same size as "Trinity", the first nuclear explosion of The United States.

THE KOREAN WAR
1950-1953

Following World War II and the end of hostilities in Asia, the United States and the Soviet Union split Korea in half. Communists controlled the North while the South became democratic. Hostilities began in the South as guerilla fighters backed by the Communists rose up against the democratic government. These groups were put down at first, but eventually the Communist North launched a full invasion.

During the invasion, the entire South Korean nation was almost completely taken over until the United Nations intervened. The United States came to the South's aid and helped push the Communists back north.

As the North slowly lost ground, their Communist Chinese allies intervened to help stop the United Nations from advancing. This invasion was eventually halted at the 38th Parallel where peace negotiations began. This line remains the border between North and South Korea to this day.

THE EAST GERMAN WORKERS' UPRISING
1953
WIR STREIKEN

What began on June 16, 1953 as an East German construction workers' strike would turn into a nationwide uprising. Three hundred construction workers went on strike to protest pay cuts. Numbers swelled throughout the day as the strike continued, and by the next day almost 40,000 protesters had taken the streets. Soviet tanks and soldiers were dispatched to quell the uprising, killing at least 55 of the protesters. Almost 2,000 were injured and over 5,000 were arrested.

THE WARSAW PACT IS SIGNED
1955

The Soviets felt threatened because West Germany had become a member of NATO. In response, on May 14, 1955, the Soviet Union and its satellite countries within Eastern Europe formed a mutual defense organization known as the Warsaw Pact. The treaty included Albania, Bulgaria, Czechoslovakia, East Germany, Hungary, Poland, Romania, and Soviet Russia.

HUNGARIAN UPRISING 1956

Students demanding political reforms began a demonstration in the streets of Budapest, Hungary. Among other things, their demands included free elections and the removal of all Soviet troops. The crowd was fired upon by State Security Police. This demonstration would become a full-scale revolution, as thousands of Hungarians from across the country took up arms against the Soviet-backed government. The Soviets would eventually invade the country, crushing the revolt. Over 2,000 Hungarians and 500 Soviet soldiers would die. Mass arrests would continue for months after the conflict, and Soviets attempted to erase the revolution from history.

SUEZ CANAL CRISIS
1956

The United Kingdom, Israel, and France attempted an invasion of Egypt to take control of the Suez Canal and to remove the Egyptian President from power. Pressure from the United States and the Soviet Union would eventually force the three aggressors to withdraw from the area.

THE SOVIET UNION LAUNCHES THE FIRST MANNED SATELLITE

1957

The United States and the Soviet Union began to compete over who was more advanced in exploring space. The Soviet Union was the first to make a major advancement with the launch of Sputnik I, the first unmanned space satellite. This would spark the United States to invest more in their space program, eventually leading to the moon landing.

1959   FIDEL CASTRO TAKES CONTROL OF CUBA

Cuba had been under the control of a U.S.- backed government led by President Fulgencio Batista. Fidel Castro began a movement within the country to take back control under a new communist leadership. As Cuba aligned itself with Communist values, it gained the support of the Soviet Union, eventually resulting in the Cuban Missile Crisis.

U2 SPY INCIDENT

1960

The U2 was a type of spy plane used by the United States to conduct covert operations. These planes would fly at a high altitude, taking photographs and conducting reconnaissance on Soviet operations. Much to the embarrassment of the United States, one of these planes was shot down by a Soviet missile on May 1, 1960, increasing tensions between the two nations. The American pilot was captured and sentenced to prison, but was released early in exchange for a captured Soviet spy.

BAY OF PIGS INVASION

APRIL 1961

On April 17, 1961, in an attempt to overthrow the communist Cuban government controlled of Fidel Castro, 1,400 American-backed Cuban exiles launched an invasion of the country. It became apparent to the rest of the world that the rebels were backed by the United States, and American President John F. Kennedy decided against further aid and air support for them. The rebels were eventually defeated in a counter attack led by Castro himself and sentenced to prison, although they were eventually released to the United States in exchange for food and medical supplies.

BERLIN WALL IS CONSTRUCTED

1961

In order to decrease the never-ending stream of refugees fleeing from East Berlin into West Berlin, the Soviet government began to build a wall around the Western half of the city. This wall would come to represent the Cold War, and as long as it stood, many East Germans would attempt to cross it and gain freedom.

CUBAN MISSILE CRISIS
OCTOBER 1962

Soviet leaders intended to install nuclear missile installations on the island of Cuba. American President Kennedy faced off against Soviet Premier Khrushchev over whether this installation would occur. In order to prevent the missiles from being installed in Cuba, the United States would enact a naval blockade surrounding the island.

As the situation developed, the possibility of nuclear war between the two nations became more and more serious. The crisis eventually ended with Kennedy promising not to invade Cuba if the Soviets would remove their nuclear missiles from the island country. President Kennedy also secretly agreed to remove American nuclear missiles stationed in Turkey.

THE VIETNAM WAR
1965-1975

The Vietnam War was a proxy war fought in the Southeast Asian country that shares its name. Communist-backed North Vietnam faced off against South Vietnam, which was supported by the United States and other democratic powers, in a bid to determine the fate of this country. The United States had been sending military advisors to aid the South since the 1950's, but the war didn't escalate until 1965, when the United States began deploying combat units to actively fight.

The Vietnam War stretched on for 10 years with no major gain for the United States, until they finally began to withdraw troops and leave the region. This phase was known as Vietnamization, which aimed to train South Vietnam to take over responsibility for its own military defense. Shortly after the United States removed itself from the conflict, South Vietnam fell to the North, and the country became communist.

PRAGUE SPRING UPRISING
1968

Attempts to pass reforms that would ensure freedoms for the people of Czechoslovakia and make the country more democratic were met with heavy resistance from the Soviet Union, who at the time was treating Czechoslovakia as a puppet state. This would eventually culminate in a Soviet invasion of the country to reverse these reforms and to reinstall a communist government that would preside over the nation.

THE UNITED STATES LANDS ON THE MOON
1969

The Soviet Union may have launched the first satellites into space, but the United States would make great leaps and bounds ahead of the Soviets in the Space Race when it landed on the moon in 1969. The Apollo 11 mission, made of up Neil Armstrong, Buzz Aldrin, and Michael Collins, would land on the moon and plant the American flag there.

DÉTENTE
1969 - 1979

After the Cuban missile crisis, the United States and the Soviet Union agreed to install a phone line directly between the two nations' capitals, so that in times of emergency they could easily and quickly communicate with each other. Following this, there would also be a reduction in weapons production, temporarily easing Cold War tensions.

SOVIETS INVADE AFGHANISTAN 1979

The Soviets invaded and staged a coup within Afghanistan in 1979, overthrowing the current Afghan president, who had been open to democratic values, and replacing him with a rival socialist leader. The invasion was immediately condemned by the rest of the world. The United States and other nations would aid insurgent forces fighting against the Soviets, but would never directly be involved.

THE BERLIN WALL COMES DOWN

1989

The leader of East Germany declared a change in relations with the Western world, announcing that East German citizens could now visit West Germany. Crowds of East Germans met at the checkpoints into West Germany and began demanding access. At first the guards were hesitant, but then began allowing the people through. With this newly found freedom of movement, the Germans began to celebrate, climbing and dancing on the wall until eventually the people began tearing it apart, representing the reunification of Germany.

THE SOVIET UNION IS ABOLISHED
1991

Mikhail Gorbachev, the leader of the Soviet Union at the time, resigned from power and handed all authority over to the new president of Russia, Boris Yeltsin. The pre-revolution Russian flag was lifted back up and the Soviet flag came down. The Soviet Union had officially abolished itself and all of the small nations under its control became sovereign once again.

COLD WAR
EXPERIENCE

COLD WAR WEAPONS

NUCLEAR MISSILES AND SUBMARINES

Nuclear weapons at the end of the World War II were not very sophisticated. They would simply be dropped from a plane, and would then parachute down to earth where they would detonate, allowing the crew of the airplane enough time to safely escape. As the arms race continued, missiles were developed to carry the nuclear payload across continents, no longer requiring a plane for delivery. Many of these weapons were transported on submarines that could fire them from the water, and slip back beneath the surface.

SPY PLANES

Aviation saw massive advancements in the Cold War, as nations tried to spy on one another from high above. The United States began the U2 program for this purpose, with planes flying high in the sky armed only with a camera. These missions were highly dangerous, as the planes carried no weapons. The United States would not officially acknowledge the existence of U2 flights, and therefore would not take responsibility for planes which were shot down.

SATELLITES

While the first satellites were very simple machines that only delivered radio signals, both the United States and the Soviet Union recognized their great potential as espionage tools. Satellites would be launched by both sides to take pictures of the enemy from high above the atmosphere.

THE BERLIN WALL

One man tightrope walked across power lines above the wall. He fell and broke some bones, but he landed on the Western half, into freedom.

In their attempts escape to West Berlin, many people were killed by East Berlin police. Barbed wire stood atop the wall, and in some sections there were even minefields in place. Anyone who attempted to escape to West Berlin was in for a very difficult and dangerous crossing.

MANY EAST GERMANS WOULD ATTEMPT TO FLEE COMMUNIST EAST GERMANY BY ESCAPING INTO WEST BERLIN. THE BERLIN WALL WAS BUILT TO SURROUND AND CUT OFF WEST BERLIN FROM THE EAST, IN ORDER TO PREVENT SUCH ESCAPES. AFTER THE RISE OF THE WALL AND THE INCREASE OF SECURITY, MANY PEOPLE TURNED TO CREATIVE AND INGENIOUS WAYS OF SCALING THE WALL.

American troops could observe, but not intervene.

Another escape was attempted by removing the windshield from a convertible. The driver sped toward the police checkpoint. Because of the height of the roadblock and how low the car sat, he was able to zoom underneath and escaped to West Berlin.

USA

HARRY S. TRUMAN
In power: 1945-1953

Truman was the president of the United States at the end of World War II, after the death of Franklin Roosevelt. He instituted the Truman Doctrine to help prevent Communism from spreading across the globe.

JOHN F. KENNEDY
In power: 1961-1963

John F. Kennedy was president of the United States during the Cuban Missile Crisis, and helped prevent the start of a nuclear war. His presidency ended when he was assassinated while riding in a motorcade in Dallas, Texas.

RICHARD NIXON
In power: 1969-1974

President Nixon ended U.S. involvement in Vietnam during the Cold War. He later would resign his office because of the Watergate Scandal.

RONALD REAGAN
In power: 1981-1989

During his presidency, Ronald Reagan was able to ease tensions between the United States and the Soviet Union, pressuring the Soviets to tear down the Berlin Wall.

JOSEPH STALIN
In power: 1929-1953

Following the reign of Vladimir Lenin, Stalin became the second leader of the Soviet Union. He led the nation through the Second World War and the reconstruction which followed. It was during his reign as dictator that tensions with Western nations began to rise.

NIKITA KHRUSHCHEV
In power: 1953-1964

As a counter to John F. Kennedy, Khrushchev led the Soviet Union through the Cuban Missile Crisis. He was a less oppressive leader than his predecessor, and even denounced Stalin as a murderer of innocent people. Under his leadership, tensions were eased and Soviet relations with the West improved.

USSR

LEONID BREZHNEV
In power: 1964-1982

Brezhnev's period of rule over the Soviet Union saw an increase in Soviet influence as he dramatically increased Soviet military strength, and pursued détente, an easing of hostility, with the Western world.

MIKHAIL GORBACHEVX
In power: 1985-1991

Gorbachev was the last leader of the Soviet Union, resigning his presidency when the Union fell. His policies of openness and reconstruction helped bring an end to tensions with the West.

Gadgets

Throughout the Cold War, spies would carry all sorts of gadgets to aid in gathering intelligence about their enemies. The bulk of what a spy would use needed to be small and concealable. Many of these items would be carried in the spy's briefcase. These would include micro cameras for taking pictures, maps, and transmitters held within shaving cream containers.

Spy Pen

Soviet spies were notorious for carrying pens with disappearing ink.

Phone bugs

Phone bugs were used to monitor telephones from an adjoining room. They could be hidden anywhere, including the heels of shoes!

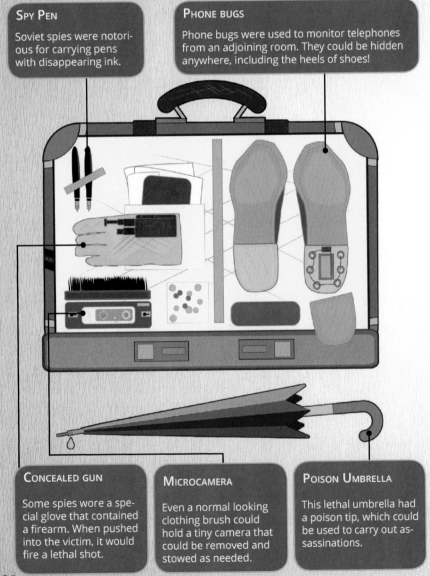

Concealed Gun

Some spies wore a special glove that contained a firearm. When pushed into the victim, it would fire a lethal shot.

Microcamera

Even a normal looking clothing brush could hold a tiny camera that could be removed and stowed as needed.

Poison Umbrella

This lethal umbrella had a poison tip, which could be used to carry out assassinations.

SPACE RACE

The Space Race was a competition between the United States and Soviet Union for supremacy in space exploration, proving which nation was more advanced and had more wealth to spend. While it wasn't a true battleground of the Cold War, up in space the two nations pushed each other to see who could go farther and higher. While the Soviets succeeded in launching Sputnik, the first artificial Earth satellite, the Apollo moon landing by the Americans was seen as a victory in this race.

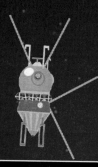

1957 - Soviet Russia launched the first Earth-orbiting satellite, Sputnik 1.

1961 - Russian cosmonaut Yuri Gagarin became the first man ever into space.

1965 - Cosmonaut Alexey Leonov performed the first space walk.

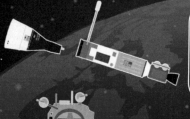

1966 - America became the first to successfully dock two space craft in orbit. On March 16th,1966 Gemini VIII, piloted by Neil Armstrong, docked with an unmanned Agena Target Vehicle.

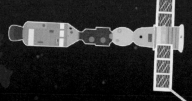

1969 - American astronauts Neil Armstrong, Michael Collins, and Buzz Aldrin become the first humans to land on the moon with the Apollo 11 mission.

1975 - The Apollo–Soyuz Test Project, a joint U.S.-Soviet space operation, became a symbol of improved American-Soviet relations. It was the first time that an American and a Russian spacecraft would dock in space.

Simple Guides

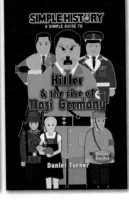

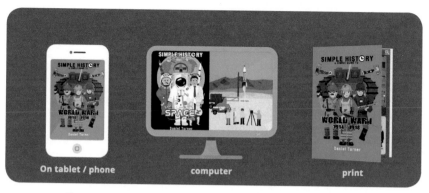

In print, tablet and e-book formats

Sign up for the mailing list for Simple History news. Simply Scan the QR code to the left with your phone.

Visit the website and social media!

www.simplehistory.co.uk

37872840R00024

Made in the USA
Lexington, KY
01 May 2019